ALL ABOUT MARY MOTHER OF JESUS

CHILDREN'S JESUS BOOK

Speedy Publishing LLC
40 E. Main St. #1156
Newark, DE 19711
www.speedypublishing.com

Let's learn about the Life of Mother Mary.

Practice writing the sentences in the space provided.

Mary was a first
century woman of
Nazareth and the
mother of Jesus.

Mary was a first
century woman of
Nazareth and the
mother of Jesus.

Christian beliefs about Mary are based on the Bible.

Christian beliefs about Mary are based on the Bible.

Mary was a young woman when she first became a mother.

Mary was a
young woman
when she first
became a mother.

Mary was
engaged to be
married to a man
called Joseph.

Mary was
engaged to be
married to a man
called Joseph.

Angel Gabriel came
to Mary to tell her
that she would give
birth to a son.

Angel Gabriel came to Mary to tell her that she would give birth to a son.

Angel Gabriel told
Mary that she
would call her
son Jesus.

Angel Gabriel told Mary that she would call her son Jesus.

Angel Gabriel said
that Jesus would
save people from
their sins.

Angel Gabriel said
that Jesus would
save people from
their sins.

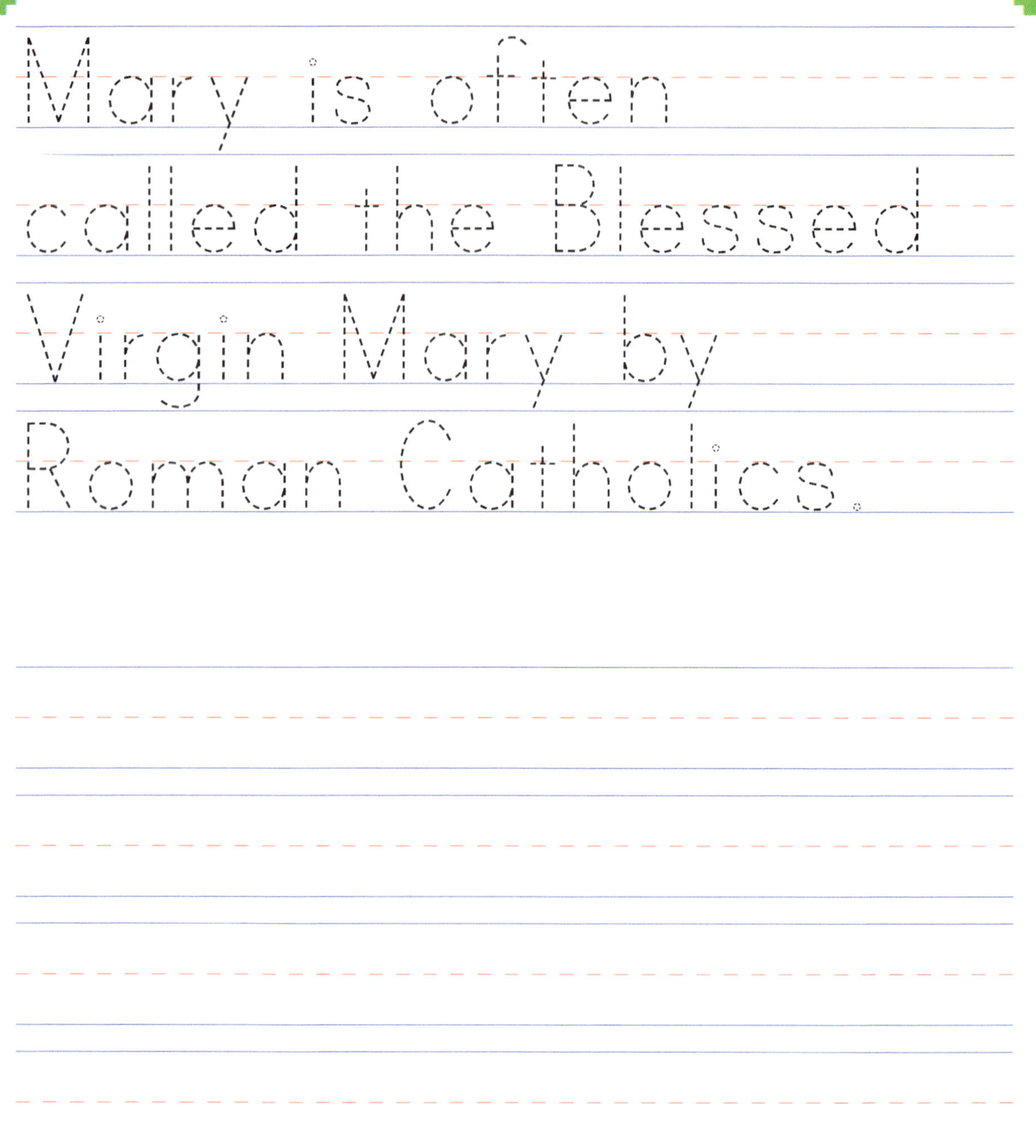
Mary is often
called the Blessed
Virgin Mary by
Roman Catholics.

Mary is often called the Blessed Virgin Mary by Roman Catholics.

God had made
Mary pregnant
through a miracle.

God had made Mary pregnant through a miracle.

Mary gave birth in a manger, because they could not find a room to stay in.

Mary gave birth in
a manger, because
they could not find a
room to stay in.

Mary and Joseph, raises Jesus the best way they could and with great love.

Mary and Joseph,
raises Jesus the best
way they could and
with great love.

Jesus spent many
happy, quiet years
with Mary and
Joseph in Nazareth.

Jesus spent many
happy, quiet years
with Mary and
Joseph in Nazareth.

When Jesus was thirty years old, he began his preaching and healing.

When Jesus was thirty years old, he began his preaching and healing.

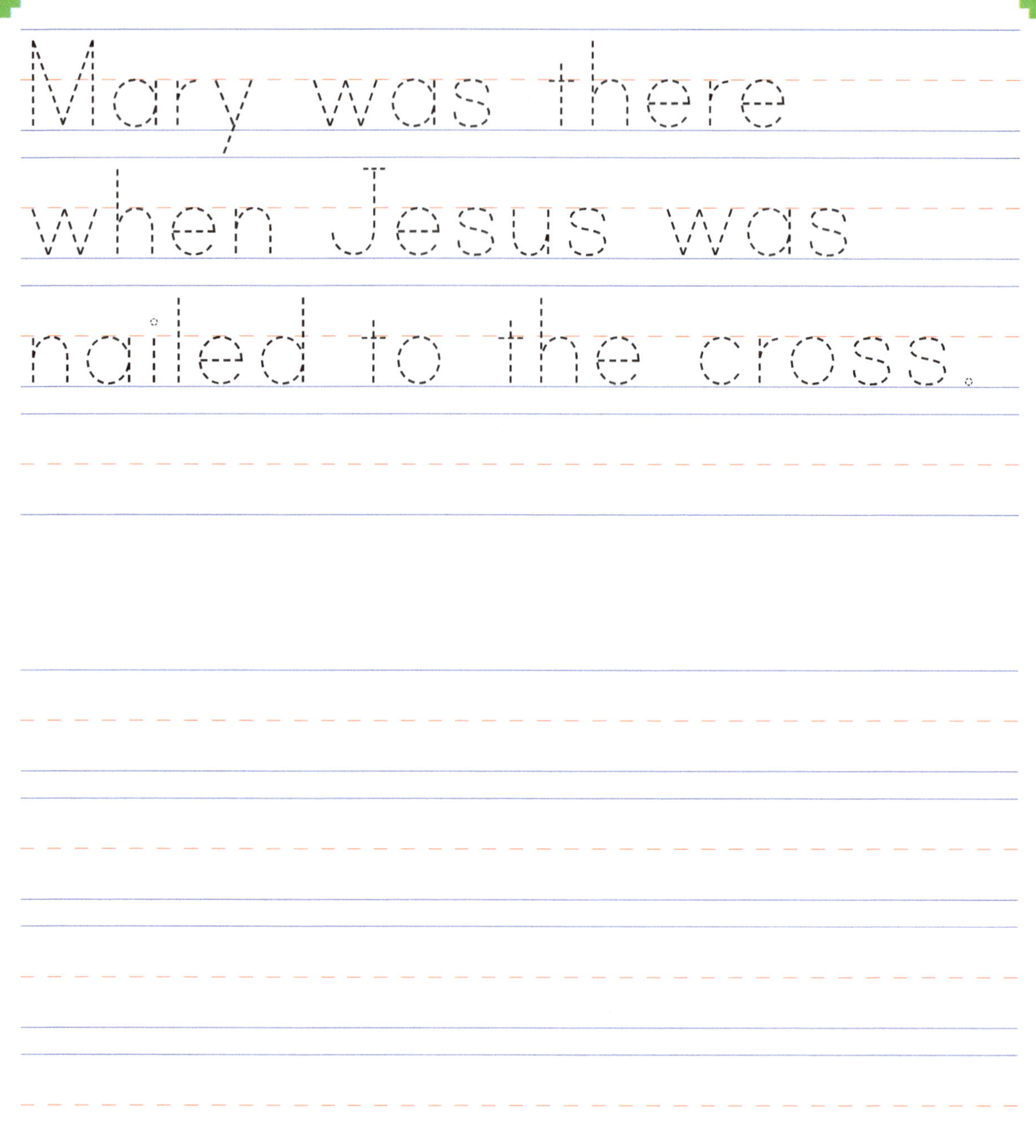

Mary was there
when Jesus was
nailed to the cross.

Mary was there
when Jesus was
nailed to the cross.

Mary stayed right
beneath the cross
and cradled the
dead body of Jesus.

Mary stayed right beneath the cross and cradled the dead body of Jesus.

Mary was a cousin of Elizabeth, wife of the priest Zechariah according to Luke.

Mary was a cousin
of Elizabeth, wife of
the priest Zechariah
according to Luke.

Mary's date of birth
is unknown but it
is celebrated every
8th of September.

Mary's date of birth
is unknown but it is
celebrated every 8th
of September.

Mary is the pre-
eminent saint and
the focus of much
popular devotion.

Mary is the pre-
eminent saint and
the focus of much
popular devotion.

www.ingramcontent.com/pod-product-compliance
Lightning Source LLC
LaVergne TN
LVHW082302150826
845677LV00009B/1701